Confidence for Men

3 Secret Hacks to Live Life on Your Terms

By

John Adams

© Copyright 2018 - All rights reserved.

The content contained within this book may not be reproduced, duplicated or transmitted without direct written permission from the author or the publisher.

Under no circumstances will any blame or legal responsibility be held against the publisher, or author, for any damages, reparation, or monetary loss due to the information contained within this book. Either directly or indirectly.

Legal Notice:

This book is copyright protected. This book is only for personal use. You cannot amend, distribute, sell, use, quote or paraphrase any part, or the content within this book, without the consent of the author or publisher.

Disclaimer Notice:

Please note the information contained within this document is for educational and entertainment purposes only. All effort has been executed to present accurate, up to date, and reliable, complete information. No warranties of any kind are declared or implied. Readers acknowledge that the author is not engaging in the rendering of legal, financial, medical or professional advice. The content within this book has been derived from various sources. Please consult a licensed professional before attempting any techniques outlined in this book.

By reading this document, the reader agrees that under no circumstances is the author responsible for any losses, direct or indirect, which are incurred as a result of the use of information contained within this document, including, but not limited to, — errors, omissions, or inaccuracies.

Table Of Contents

Chapter 1: Introduction – Understanding Confidence   7

   Why is Confidence Important?   9

   Is Confidence a Genetically Acquired or Learned Skill?   12

   Confidence and Assertiveness   14

   Confidence and Self-Esteem   15

   Chapter Summary   16

Chapter 2: Understanding Your Current Level of Confidence   17

Chapter 3: How to Start Being Confident   27

   Growth Mindset   27

   Fixed Mindset Triggers and How to Avoid Them   29

   Learning and Practicing New Skills Until You Master Them   34

   Chapter Summary   35

Chapter 4: Self-Awareness - Know Your Core Values   37

   Importance of Core Values   38

   Characteristics of Core Values   40

   Chapter Summary   45

Chapter 5: Setting Goals; Your Mission and Purpose   47

   Why is Goal-Setting Important?   47

   Chapter Summary   54

Chapter 6: Tips and Tricks to Build Confidence - Part I   55

   Building Confidence through Visualizations   55

   Confidence Building through Affirmations   58

   Challenge Yourself Continuously   61

   Journals for Confidence Building   63

Chapter Summary ... 66
Chapter 7: Tips and Tricks to Build Confidence - Part II ... **67**
Avoid Perfectionism ... 67
Love Yourself ... 71
Have a Positive Attitude ... 73
Chapter Summary ... 75
Chapter 8: Conclusion ... **77**

Chapter 1: Introduction – Understanding Confidence

Confidence is the measure of your belief in your own strengths and the identification and acceptance of your weaknesses. A confident man is one who knows the real value of his capabilities and uses them with pride and humbly accepts his drawbacks without being overwhelmed. He feels secure in this knowledge and does not allow his sense of confidence-backed pride to turn to arrogance. A confident man, therefore:

- Has a healthy level of self-worth
- Has a powerful sense of certainty and self-assuredness about his own abilities
- Has faith and trust in himself, and in others
- Is ever-ready to adapt to changing situations
- Is always optimistic and has a clearly-defined set of goals
- Is self-aware and feels motivated to work towards his goals

'A confident man is not one who is always right, but, one who is not afraid of being wrong,' is one the aptest quotes to define confidence.

Another way to understand confidence is by relating it to low self-esteem and arrogance. Confidence comes from knowing and appreciating your strengths and their real value. Contrarily, arrogance comes because you think you are more valuable than you really are, and low self-esteem comes because you think you are less valuable than you really are.

Confidence is not always about winning. Do you remember the movie *Rocky*? Does the protagonist, Rocky Balboa, win the final fight? No, it ends in a draw. However, people don't really remember the result. They only remember the confidence with which Stallone's character went through all the 15 rounds, never giving up at any time. That is confidence; to continue to battle it out even if you think you might lose.

Also, there is a subtle difference between having confidence and being confident. Having confidence is based on your inner strengths and capabilities while being confident is about appearing confident in front of other people. Typically, people who have confidence present a confident profile to the outside world naturally.

However, there are multiple instances wherein some men appear confident even though they don't feel it inside. This conflict can last for a little while, but, after some time, your lack of confidence within yourself will reflect on the outside as well.

Real confidence is quiet and unpretentious. However, when a confident man walks into a room, everyone can feel it.

Why is Confidence Important?

Being confident comes with multiple benefits, and some of them are listed below. However, you must remember that this personality trait is not 'right' or 'wrong.' Don't judge yourself and feel ashamed or guilty if you lack confidence.

First, accept yourself the way you are, and then learn the tricks and tips to build this critical personality trait to leverage its many benefits. The Dalai Lama says, *'A man cannot make peace with the outside world if he hasn't made peace with himself.'*

Look at the life history of James Eugene Carrey, or more famously Jim Carrey. He had a tough childhood when his musician father lost his job, and poverty reared its ugly head in his family. He quit studying at the age of 15 and started working as a janitor to help increase his family's income.

Despite all odds, his passion and confidence in his comic abilities never left him at all. And yet, his debut comedy show was a big flop. But, that didn't deter him. Jim Carrey persisted in his efforts driven by his confidence in himself and his capabilities. His story is a classic example of leveraging the power of confidence to achieve success, despite early setbacks.

Here are some excellent reasons why you should endeavor to build and develop your confidence levels:

You will have a healthy level of self-esteem – When you are confident, you have learned to accept your strengths and weaknesses realistically. You value your capabilities and humbly accept your weaknesses, thereby empowering you to walk with your head held high wherever you go.

For example, suppose you worked hard on a presentation and confidently presented it to your colleagues and seniors in your office. Words of praise for your work will take your confidence and self-esteem levels a few notches up.

Your days will be filled with increased levels of happiness and joy – With increased confidence and self-esteem, you are bound to achieve a lot more success than before. These successes bring a lot of happiness and joy to your life.

For example, if you have not been achieving good sales numbers for two weeks, but have persisted in your efforts consistently and confidently, sales numbers are bound to come sooner rather than later. And when they start coming, the compliments from your boss and the incentives will give you and your family a lot of happiness and joy.

Your capabilities and strengths will get better with increasing confidence – Increased confidence results in improved self-worth and a lot of successes which, in turn, motivate you to upskill yourself and get better at your strengths and capabilities. Each new challenge you encounter will teach you innovative lessons which, in turn, will help build and develop your skills and abilities. Moreover, these challenges can also serve to overcome your weaknesses as you develop your learning.

For example, as you build confidence and get more sales to your credit, you will find ways and means to get better by upskilling yourself through various online courses or attending training sessions or reading books to improve your salesmanship. Success from confident efforts drives you to self-improvement.

You will lose your self-doubting nature – We are all self-doubting naturally because we are uncertain of what to expect, and even more uncertain of whether we can do what we should be doing in a particular situation. As you build confidence and taste the success of your efforts, your self-doubting nature will slowly reduce, and with persistent efforts, will almost disappear. One of the primary reasons for reduced self-doubt is the fact that you realize that confidence comes from accepting failures with equanimity.

Confidence is one of the most attractive qualities in men – Women in particular, and all people in general, find confident men very attractive. Here are some great reasons for that:

- Confident men can handle any situation well. Even in failed situations, you will find confident men giving their most radiant smile reflective of their humble acceptance of defeat, and manfully congratulating the winners.
- Confident men are positive thinkers. No matter how bad a situation might look, confident men will find a positive element in it, and take the forward path from there, and move ahead
- Confident men are powerful leaders who achieve amazing popularity amongst their followers
- Confident men are happy and comfortable being themselves
- Confident men build faith and trust; key elements for people to feel attraction

With so many benefits on offer, it makes sense to work hard to build your level of confidence.

Is Confidence a Genetically Acquired or Learned Skill?

This is a very pertinent question for modern times because, until recently, one of the most popular tenets was that confident men are born, not made. A son of a confident man is confident, and the son of a not-so-confident man is born with little or no confidence. However, nothing can be farther from the truth than this misconception.

For, if this was true, then the son of Abraham Lincoln should have been equally famous as his father. Nelson Mandela's children should have had the same level of confidence that their father had. This does not mean to say that the children of these famous people lacked confidence. However, they were not able to display it at the same level as their fathers did, right?

Biological factors are important to the extent that if you are genetically predisposed to being more confident, building the necessary skills might be easier for you than for someone who is not genetically predisposed in this manner. However, our destinies are not decided by our genes.

Taking the same examples as above, neither Abraham Lincoln's nor Nelson Mandela's father achieved the level of confidence that their sons achieved. Therefore, confidence is a skill that can be learned and mastered and not something that is necessarily acquired genetically.

Building confidence is a matter of developing good habits, creating the right mindset, and working hard towards self-improvement. Here are some more classic examples of people who did all these things, and became super-confident in their lives:

Jeff Bezos – Today, he is one of the richest men on earth. However, he didn't start like that. He simply believed in his vision and capabilities and built an e-commerce industry more than 20 years ago at a time when very few people in the world believed in the power of this market. He continues to innovate his dreams and visions despite achieving amazing success.

Stephen King – This celebrated author was rejected 60 times before he found a publisher who believed in his work. In fact, King wore borrowed clothes for his wedding, and yet nothing stopped him from being confident in his capabilities. He endeavored relentlessly with the support of that belief and achieved amazing success.

Confidence and Assertiveness

Assertive and confidence complement each other. Your confidence comes through when you are assertive, and when you are confident, your assertiveness levels are high.

Yet, there are differences between the two traits. You don't need an external audience to have and feel confident. It's an internal element of your personality that is reflected in your behavior naturally.

However, to be assertive, you need an external audience who form the target of your assertive behavior. There must be some people or person to whom you have to show your assertiveness skills. It is based on perception.

A genuine, deep-rooted reflection of confidence comes out in the form of powerful assertive behavior.

Confidence and Self-Esteem

Self-esteem and confidence are similar traits and are often employed interchangeably. The two traits are connected in the sense that they are directly proportional to each other. And yet, there are differences.

Self-esteem is more or less the same in all aspects of your life. Say, for example, you have high self-esteem in your workplace. Then, it is very likely that you have high self-esteem in your personal life. It is unusual for someone to feel worthy of himself at the office, and unworthy of himself at home, or vice versa. Self-esteem is nothing but the sense of self-worth you possess. Confidence, on the other hand, can vary across different aspects of your life. For example, you could be a confident professional in your workplace because you have excellent professional skills. However, at home, your confidence level as a father could be quite low because you are uncertain of your parenting skills.

Moreover, confidence is an easier trait to build than self-esteem. Confidence can be easily linked to tangible elements as the skills learned, the outcomes of your efforts, the success achieved, etc. Contrarily, self-esteem is an intangible trait that you must feel within yourself, which is more difficult to understand and build.

Chapter Summary

In this chapter, you learned that confidence is a measure of your self-awareness including your strengths and weaknesses without any underlying arrogance. You also learned the multiple benefits of building confidence, and how it is not as much a genetic skill as it is a learned skill. Anyone can learn and master the art of confidence. You also learned how confidence is linked to assertiveness and self-esteem.

Chapter 2: Understanding Your Current Level of Confidence

Identifying your current level of confidence is the best way to take your confidence-building journey forward. Therefore, this chapter is dedicated to a self-discovery questionnaire and a partner-based self-discovery discussion to help you do just that.

Q1. When my boss gives me a tricky problem to solve, I am confident I can use my professional capabilities to find suitable solutions.
1. Never   2. Sometimes   3. Very often   4. Always

Q2. Using my technical and soft skills, I am confident I can do a great job in my workplace.
1. Never   2. Sometimes   3. Very often   4. Always

Q3. I have always tested my theoretical skills with practical applications.
1. Never   2. Sometimes   3. Very often   4. Always

Q4. I can confidently lead a team to run a challenging project.
1. Never   2. Sometimes   3. Very often   4. Always

Q5. When my team-members come to me with problems, and even though I may not have a solution immediately for them, I am confident to know where to look for the answers.
1. Never   2. Sometimes   3. Very often   4. Always

Q6. I can confidently explain complex theories to my colleagues, team members, and even seniors.
1. Never   2. Sometimes   3. Very often   4. Always

Q7. I am confident of getting my promotions and salary increases based on my performance.
1. Never   2. Sometimes   3. Very often   4. Always

Q8. Would you consider appearing in a TV reality quiz show?
1. Yes   2. I don't know   3. No

Q9. If you are asked to give a long speech about your friend at his wedding, will you accept the task?
1. Yes   2. I don't know   3. No

Q10. Do you believe you are basically a positive individual?
1. Yes   2. I don't know   3. No

Q11. If you were given a choice and you had the necessary skills, would you pilot a plane with over 100 passengers traveling in it?
1. Yes   2. I don't know   3. No

Q12. Would you like to meet high profile and famous people on a one-to-one basis and ask them questions?
1. Yes   2. I am not interested   3. No

Q13. Have you had disagreements with your boss?
1. Yes, Many times   2. A couple of times   3. No, not at all

Q14. Are you comfortable being in front of your friends in swimming trunks?
1. Yes   2. Only with certain people   3. No

Q15. If you were caught by a traffic warden and charged a penalty for an offense, would you contradict him if you believed you were not wrong?
1. Yes   2. I don't know   3. No

Q16. Do you believe in the adage, 'Attack is the best form of defense?'
1. Yes   2. Only sometimes   3. No

Q17. Are you comfortable driving in bad and chaotic traffic?
1. Yes   2. I don't know   3. No

Q18. Are you confident while crossing the road?
1. Yes   2. Not on certain roads   3. No

Q19. If there was a warning of a storm, would you still take the ferry?
1. Yes   2. For an emergency only   3. No

Q20. Do you recall an incident in your life which in retrospect makes you feel you were ruthless?
1. Yes, many   2. Just 1-2   3. No

Q21. Are you impressed by powerful people?
1. Yes   2. No   3. Not often

Q22. Are you someone who ignores warning signs?
1. Yes   2. For an emergency only   3. No

Q23. If you were to choose between two projects, and one was clearly more difficult than the other, would you opt for the difficult one?
1. Yes   2. I don't know   3. No

Q24. Do you believe your intelligence level is above the average person's?
1. Yes   2. I don't know   3. No

Q25. Would you act in a play?
1. Yes   2. I don't know   3. No

Q26. Would you like to train to become a rally car driver?

1. Yes   2. I don't know   3. No

Q27. Would you participate in a dare with your friends to walk through a cemetery in the dead of night?

1. Yes   2. I don't know   3. No

Q28. Are you confident of flying in a small twin-prop engine airplane?

1. Yes   2. I don't know   3. No

Q29. Would you like to stand for election?

1. Yes   2. I don't know   3. No

Q30. Would you walk on a tightrope in a game of dare?

1. Yes   2. I don't know   3. No

Q31. If you are alone at home, and you hear a sound in the kitchen at night, would you get up to go check?

1. Yes   2. I don't know   3. No

Q32. Do you think you are better than most people in your professional and personal social circles?

1. Yes   2. I don't know   3. No

Q33. Do other people's opinions worry or bother you?

1. Yes   2. Sometimes, if the person is someone I care about   3. No

Q34. Are you excessively sensitive to criticism?
1. Yes   2. Sometimes, if the criticizer is my rival   3. No

Q35. Do you feel nervous in front of your boss and those people whose opinions you value?
1. Yes   2. Sometimes, if the outcome is dependent on their opinions   3. No

Q36. Do you think positively about yourself?
1. Always   2. Quite often   3. Rarely   4. Never

Q37. When you are talking to people, do you feel comfortable maintaining eye contact?
1. Always   2. Quite often   3. Rarely   4. Never

Q38. Do you get nervous if you have to speak in front of strangers?
1. Yes   2. I don't know, haven't got an opportunity   3. No

Q39. Do you get nervous if you have to speak in front of family and friends, like at a friend's wedding or a family function?
1. Yes   2. I don't know, I have never been asked to   3.

No

Q40. Are you happy with the way you are as a person?
1. Yes   2. Not really, I could have been better   3. No, not at all

Q41. Do you always need external validation to feel good about yourself?
1. Yes   2. I don't know   3. No

Confidence-Gauging Exercise with a Partner

Taking the help of a confidante is another excellent way to arrive at your present levels of confidence. In fact, you and your friend can use this exercise for self-discovery: one helping the other. Now, both imagine a situation which calls for a deep level of confidence.

For example, you can think of giving an impromptu speech at your friend's wedding. Now, both complete this questionnaire based on that imagined situation. For the time being, leave the space for 'friend's comment' blank.

Q1. What do you think will be your emotions? Will it be fear, confidence, or something else?

_____

_____

Friend's comments

_____

_____

Q2. How do you think you will manage your feelings at such a time?

_____

_____

Friend's comments

_____

_____

Q3. What will be your level of preparedness? Will such an impromptu demand on you excite you or drive you into a panic mode?

_____

_____

Friend's comments

_____

_____

Q4. Suppose the audience consisted of only very close family and friends, would your answers be different?

_____

_____

Friend's comments

_____

_____

When both of you have finished the exercise, exchange your notes with your friend. Now, read each other's notes, and make comments in the space for 'friend's comments.' Do you agree with your friend's comments on himself for each of the questions? Has he left out some aspect of his personality which could help you in the situation? Are your views very different from what he believes in himself? Let your friend do the same for you.

This exercise will let you know if what you believe about yourself is what comes across to other people too. For example, suppose your answer to Q1 was, 'I would feel scared and nervous,' and your friend said, 'Not at all, you are a confident person, and you will handle this situation perfectly.'

This means you come across as far more confident than you or, alternatively, you don't believe in your own capabilities as much as others do. This means you are not really self-aware, and your outside profile does not reflect your true inner self. In such conflicting circumstances, ask yourself some more questions to improve self-awareness:

Am I underestimating or overestimating my skills?

Why do I see myself differently from the way others see me?

With the results of these two answers, you will have a reasonably good idea of your current level of confidence, and you can start your development journey from there.

Chapter 3: How to Start Being Confident

The best place to start your journey of building confidence is to make the decision, "I am confident today, and I will be confident every day from now." The decision to change should come first. The other steps will follow naturally. Robert Colliers, one of the most popular writers of self-help books in the 20th century said, *'Take the first step, and your mind will mobilize all its forces to your aid. But the first essential is that you begin. Once the battle is startled, all that is within and without you will come to your assistance.'*

On that note, let us look at two important elements to build your confidence.

They are:
- Growth mindset
- Learning and practicing new skills until you master them

Growth Mindset

So, you have made the decision to start being confident from this moment, and you have taken the first, perhaps most difficult, step. Yet, the path of confidence-building is full of obstacles and challenges, and it is easy to give up on your efforts.

Your confidence level will keep fluctuating depending on multiple factors including your moods, external circumstances, health, and many more reasons. It is imperative that you develop a growth mindset to overcome these challenges and continue relentlessly on your confidence-building journey.

So, what is a growth mindset? Carol S. Dweck, a world-famous psychology professor and researcher, is credited with coining two terms associated with mindset, namely growth mindset and fixed mindset. A man with a fixed mindset believes that his capabilities, his beliefs, his mistakes, the view of the outside world towards himself, and everything else in his life is fixed. Such a man believes that changes, especially growth, are not possible.

If, for example, Bill Gates had had his mindset, then he would have given up after his initial business attempt to create meaningful reports for roadways engineers using raw data failed. Luckily for the world, Bill Gates had a growth mindset. He believed that capabilities, beliefs, mistakes, and everything else in the world are not cast in stone. Anyone with commitment to hard work and persistent efforts and a willingness to learn and grow can overcome challenges and become successful. Today, his success, thanks to his growth mindset, is there for the world to see and try to emulate.

Fixed Mindset Triggers and How to Avoid Them

So, how do you develop a growth mindset to learn new skills and achieve confidence? The first step is to avoid the traps and triggers of a fixed mindset. Along with each of the triggers mentioned, there are growth mindset thoughts and options given for your benefit.

Fixed mindset thought trigger #1 – I cannot develop and build confidence because I am already low on confidence. A growth mindset thinker will, instead, say to himself, "Yes, I am low on confidence right now. However, let me find ways and means to bring it up to scale. Whose help can I take? Are there self-help books available? Can I find a role model whom I can emulate to build confidence? I am certain that if I put in the right kind of efforts to seek help, I can easily develop my confidence, and achieve success."

Fixed mindset thought trigger #2 – I am worried about how I will be perceived by others. Contrary to being obsessed by how others perceive him, a 'growth mindset' man will think like this, "I am unique, and I will show my authentic self to people. It does not matter how I am seen as long as I live my life on my terms."

When you have thought, nothing can stop you from building confidence. You accept and love yourself the way you are. What others think of you should not stop you from doing what you want. Lao Tzu said, *"If you begin to care about what others think of you, you will always remain their prisoner."*

The obsession for 'being perceived right' not only prevents you from achieving your goals but can also drive you insane. Be wary of this important trigger and avoid it completely. Be proud of who you are because as Dr. Seuss said, *"Be who you are, and say what you want to say because those who mind don't matter, and those who matter don't mind."*

Fixed mindset thought trigger #3 – I don't want to try this because what if I fail? Growth mindset thoughts will run something like this: "I have no problem if I fail because if I didn't try, how will I know if I can do it?" Success is almost impossible with encountering failures.

It could be multiple failures like those faced by Thomas Edison (and he said of his 10,000 failures, *"I have not failed 10,000 times. I have only found 10,000 ways how not to do it"*) or it could be one epic failure that stands out like a sore thumb in your life. Failures are the biggest teachers and being scared and running away from them is not just futile but a big deterrent to success and happiness. The only way you can avoid failure is by doing nothing, saying, and being nothing, and that is definitely not living!

Here are some excellent reasons for you to treat failures and mistakes as learning and growing opportunities instead of trying to run away from them:

Mistakes drive our learning – Yes, making mistakes hurt, at least initially. But after that, your brain goes into overdrive and wants to understand what went wrong and find ways and means to correct them. The pain from the mistakes facilitates improved learning because we absorb information much better in this situation than when we are comfortable without the pain.

Mistakes drive self-compassion – We feel sorry and compassionate towards ourselves when we commit errors. This attitude increases our compassion for other people too. Moreover, multiple research studies have proven that compassionate acceptance of our mistakes drives our determination and enthusiasm to learn and improve our skills.

Mistakes free us from limiting fears and empowers us to take calculated risks – After our mistakes come to light, we lose our fear of them. We are freed from these limiting emotions that deter us from taking calculated risks in new and hitherto unchartered territories, giving us opportunities to improve confidence because success lies on the other side of fear.

Mistakes improve motivation – Hitting a big snag in our lives can wake us up from our reverie of comfort driving us to work hard and refresh our commitments to our goals.

Mistakes keep us grounded and humble – An attitude of arrogance is one of the primary adversaries of success. Mistakes help keep this debilitating attitude at bay by reminding us of our vulnerabilities. Mistakes, thus, keep us grounded and humble, which are key elements for success.

Therefore, it is important to remember that life experiences can only result in learning, or winning and not failing.

Fixed mindset thought trigger #4 – I have tried once, and I have failed. I cannot get this right. Giving up easily is one of the biggest drawbacks of having a fixed mindset. A man empowered with a growth mindset will never give up. He will persist because he believes he is on the right track. Temporary setbacks don't deter men with a growth mindset. You must remember nearly all things worthy on this earth don't come easily. Persistence and patience are vital to obtaining worthy elements in life.

Fixed mindset thought trigger #5 – If I have to try so hard, then I don't have the talent for it. Fixed mindset men believe that talented people need not put in efforts and hard work for success. It should come naturally to them. This is a complete myth, and talent is often overrated.

Growth mindset men, on the contrary, know that a great amount of talent without hard work will get you nothing, whereas the basic aptitude for a skill combined with oodles of hard work and commitment can result in outstanding success.

George O' Dowd, better known by his stage name Boy George, was rejected for his 'lack of talent.' That hardly deterred the man who worked hard at his music skills and was able to set a new hip trend in the world of pop music.

Fixed mindset thought trigger #6 – I will not listen to negative feedback because I don't need it. A fixed mindset person is never ready to accept criticism and take feedback with an intention to use it for self-improvement. He will simply ignore it, or worse still, argue with the person giving the feedback.

On the contrary, a man with growth mindset knows and accepts that feedback and criticisms are critical for self-improvement, and he will take them in the right spirit using the useful ones to get better and discarding the spiteful and useless ones.

Learning and Practicing New Skills Until You Master Them

A crucial reason for low levels of confidence is the lack of or insufficient skills. Therefore, it is important to identify critical skills that add value to your life and bring success and happiness. Once you have identified the list of important skills, you must endeavor to build and practice each of those skills until you become a master at it. Here are some tips to help you build new skills and continue learning new things:

Have a curious attitude – Always be interested in knowing how, why, what, why not, etc. A curious attitude is perfect to increase your knowledge and skills. A curious learner imbibes knowledge quickly and effectively. Look at children and learn from their limitless curiosity.

Improve your versatility – When you are good at many things or can have meaningful conversations with different groups of people, your confidence level is bound to get a boost as more people will appreciate your knowledge and skills. Don't hesitate to learn new skills at all times.

Chapter Summary

In this chapter, you learned the importance of growth mindset to build confidence. You also learned tips and tricks on how to have a growth mindset and how to practice a new skill until you become a master at it.

Chapter 4: Self-Awareness - Know Your Core Values

What are core values and why are they important in your life? This is the best way to make a list of your core values based on which you will lead your life.

So, what are core values? We value a lot of things and people in our lives. For example, you could value your home, your wife, kids, parents, teachers, your job, your friends, etc. Many of your choices in life are based on the priorities you give to the people and things you value.

For instance, suppose you have to choose between going to work on a weekend to complete an important project with a deadline coming up very soon and taking your kids out on a picnic that you promised last week. Your choice will depend on the value you have given to your kids and your job.

Which is more important in your life? What makes your life worthwhile? Your choices are founded on those priorities. Remember there are no right or wrong answers. They are a reflection of which values are important to you and how you rank them in your life, that's all. Like Elvis Presley said, *"Values are like fingerprints. Nobody's are the same as anyone else's;*

but you leave them all over everything you do."

Core values are qualities or traits that guide and drive your life and life choices. Core values not only help you live a happy life but also give you valid reasons to make the right decisions so that you lead a fulfilling and meaningful life.

Importance of Core Values

Core values give you a sense of purpose – Most of us don't really have a purpose in life. We drift along going where our lives take us, uncertain of where we want to reach. Only when you know what is important in your life can you know what you want from it. Core values help you understand your priorities in life.

Core values help you make the right choices in difficult situations – Core values become our guiding principles in life and help us make the right choice in difficult situations. You can easily align your behavior with your core values. Core values, therefore, are a beacon to show you the path of your life.

Moreover, when you are stuck in a dilemma, and are unsure what you need to do, core values will shed light on the darkness. They will tell you whether you should apologize in a particular situation and back off or stand your ground and fight for your rights. For example, in the example given above, when you had to choose between your kids and office work, your core values will help you decide what comes first in this situation.

Core values help you clear off all kinds of clutter from your life – With your core values in place, you can get rid of all other things that are not aligned to them and clear your life of all kinds of clutter keeping it simple and minimalistic. The modern world consumes your life in so many ways, including social media, television media, print media, internet, and others that can lead to a feeling of claustrophobia. Clearing clutter will give your life a semblance of order.

Core values help you make the right career choice – No career is perfect. Every career has its pros and cons. With the right set of core values to guide you, you can make the right career choice that is aligned with your life goals and missions.

For example, if you value family more than anything else, then you could choose a career that gives you the flexibility of working from home. Contrarily, if you love traveling and adventure, you could choose a job that entails both these elements. Many times, identifying and developing a deep connection with your core values might give you an idea if a promotion is worth it or not!

Core values increase your level of confidence – Core values give your life a sense of certainty and stability which, in turn, helps to build your level of confidence. When you are clear about your needs, it doesn't matter what people want. You will confidently work to fulfill your needs.

Characteristics of Core Values

There are over 400 core values you can choose from. Before we go into a self-exploratory exercise on how to identify your personal core values, let us understand the basic characteristics that define core values.

Core values should be implementable in all conditions of your life – For example, honesty is a core value that you can implement no matter what condition you are in. You could be young, old, or in a wheelchair, bedridden, or anywhere else or any other state. You can still remain honest.

However, if you choose physical fitness, then this is not possible in all conditions of your life. In your bedridden state or on a wheelchair, maintaining physical fitness can be quite a challenge.

Practicing your core values should not depend on any external factor – If you choose popularity as one of your core values, then you need other people to like you in order to be popular. Therefore, this cannot be a core value in your life. But, courage or discipline does not depend on any other factor to help you implement and follow in your life.

Self-Assessment Exercise to Arrive at Your Core Values

One way of creating core values that you think worthwhile is to look at the list of over 400 available on the internet and choose from there. Some of them include adventure, freedom, ambition, family, integrity, courage, respect, fun, money, health, and many, many more.

However, the best way to make your core values list is to examine your life and your experiences and see what helped you grow and become a better individual, and what prevented you from growing and getting better. From these experiences, you can cull your list of personal core values.

Before you start this exercise, grab a pen and a notebook, and a few sticky notes to pen down your thoughts as they come to you. And give yourself at least an hour to complete this exercise satisfactorily. Now, write down answers to these questions:

Step 1: What were the best experiences in your life? Choose between 3-5 experiences that you believe made you the happiest and gave you a deep sense of satisfaction. Write answers to the following questions for each of those experiences:

Describe the experience in detail including when it happened, how old you were, what happened, and other factual details.

_____

_____

Write the most significant emotions you felt at that time. Strangely, you will notice that such powerful experiences bring back that rush of emotion, even now. Use that to make detailed notes.

_____

_____

What were the core values that were being played out in those experiences? If the experience took place many years ago, maybe when you were a child, you may not have understood what core values were at that time. Now, however, when you recall those past experiences, you will be able to clearly label the core values that stood out during the event.

_____

_____

Step 2: In the same way, recall and write down the worst experiences of your life, and answer the following questions:
Describe the experience in detail including when it happened,

how old you were, what happened, and other factual details.

_____

_____

Write the most significant emotions you felt at that time.

_____

_____

What were the core values that were being stifled out in those experiences?

_____

_____

Step 3: Define your code of conduct. To do this, you have to reflect deeply, and think of those elements in your life that come immediately after your basic survival needs are met. These elements are those that add meaning and joy to your life, and in their absence, you live life like an automaton. Some examples include:
- Adventure
- Freedom
- Health and vitality
- Learning and growth
- Creativity

Step 4: Collect all the core values you got from the answers to the above questions and combine similar core values together. For instance, you can combine productivity, efficiency, ambition, accomplishment, etc. under career. You can combine generosity, altruism, helpful, doing good to others, etc. under service-oriented.

If it is a long list, then you need to pick the top 5-10 from this list. Keeping less than 5 items in your core values list might not cover all the important tenets of life and keeping more than 10 items might create challenges for you to work with practically.

The last thing you must do is prioritize your core values in order of importance in your life. Although this activity appears simple, it could take a while. How do you rank elements that look equally important? Revisit your best and worst experiences and see if you can recall the intensity of the emotions in each of those cases. The more the intensity, the deeper you felt about that particular core value. Using the data from this exercise, you might be able to rank your core values list in order of importance.

Keep sticky notes of your core values and put them all over so that you read them daily and imbibe them deeply in your psyche.

Chapter Summary

In this chapter, you learned the definition, significance, and characteristic features of core values. Complete the experience-based exercise to arrive at your own core values.

Chapter 5: Setting Goals; Your Mission and Purpose

Your core values are in place, and they are deeply imbibed in your psyche. The next thing to do is set goals for your life. A life mission gives you purpose in life, and when you walk the goal path supported by your core values, you will be able to lead a more fulfilling and meaningful life.

Why is Goal-Setting Important?

"If you want to be happy, set a goal that commands your thoughts, liberates your energy and inspires your hopes," said Andrew Carnegie. Here are some amazing reasons why you must start setting goals today:

Goal-setting helps you achieve faster and effective results – When you have clear goals in place, you can focus on how to achieve them and not waste your time and energy focusing on what you want to achieve. With clear goals, you can work slowly daily and make certain progress towards your goal each day. As you achieve each day's goal, you will find the motivation to work hard for the next day's goal, ensuring you are making daily progress.

Clear goals improve positive attitude – Goals have the power to drive you to achieve them and put you firmly in the driver's seat. Goals are what make your dream tangible targets that can be made into daily, weekly, and monthly goals, giving you the satisfaction of achieving a little at a time. This achievement nurtures positivity in your life.

Goals prevent procrastination – Procrastination is a debilitating habit and is one of the biggest hurdles to advancement and growth. Your sense of focus and purpose is significantly improved with goal-setting, which, in turn, ensures you don't allow yourself to get into a procrastination mode. Moreover, as you break your large and long-term goals into smaller ones achievable over a shorter period, you will find it easy to do what is necessary for each little advancement without procrastinating.

Goals improve time management – Knowing exactly what you want and by when you want it ensures you don't waste time on unproductive work. You will be able to manage your time more effectively than if you didn't have clear-set goals.

Goals prevent you from getting distracted – Goals are your self-imposed boundaries keeping you on your chosen path that is moving towards your purpose. Deep-seated goals ensure your mind is quickly attuned to distractions and gives you a warning signal if you think of straying from your path.

Here is a simple example of the power of goal-setting. Suppose you had a meeting with your boss at 10 in the morning. You know you have a 15-minute walk from the station to your office. You will ensure that you get the earlier train that day and walk briskly from the station, making sure you are focused on the walk and are not distracted by anything including the coffee shop that you usually stop by for your second cup of coffee.

When your mind imbibes the power of a simple goal such as meeting with your boss and keeps you safe from distractions, you can only imagine how much more aware it will be when you have large goals deeply imbibed in your psyche.

Goals facilitate improved decision-making abilities – Every time you have to make a choice or take a decision, all you need to do is ask yourself: "Does this help you get closer to my goals or not?" You can make sensible decisions depending on the answer you get.

For example, if you have a goal of completing the presentation by the end of the day, and your friends call you to watch a game on TV, ask yourself, "What will help you reach my predetermined goal?" Then, you will find it easy to say no to your friends because that choice clearly takes you further away from your daily goal. Therefore, goals help you say NO firmly and assertively.

Self-Discovery Questions for Goal-Setting

Before you set goals based on your core values, you must know what kind of goals you must set. And for that, you need to be indulge in self-exploratory exercises to understand what you want from your life. Reflect on the following questions and write down your answers:

Q1. What is your definition of a meaningful life? If you think this question is very broad-based, break it up into the following questions:

- What moves you to work hard and drive myself?
- What motivates you?
- What are your desires?
- What are the things you care deeply about?

_____

_____

Q2. What was your position in your life previous to now? What are your past experiences? Write down both good and bad experiences. Using the memories, you can get an idea of where you were before now.

_____

_____

Q3. Where do you stand today? Use the following questions to get insights for this aspect of your self-discovery process:

- What kind of a person are you?
- What are your capabilities?
- What are your weaknesses?
- What do you love doing?
- What do you hate doing?

_____

_____

Q4. Where do you want to be 10 years from now? The answers to this question will give you an idea of where to begin your goal-setting process. To get a complete understanding of your goals, find answers to the following questions:

- What are the skills and abilities you want to build?
- What are the money and wealth goals I have?
- From a career perspective, what position do you want to reach?
- What kind of future do you envision for your loved ones?

_____

_____

Q5. Here some the specific goal-setting questions. Indulge in a little bit of self-reflection and find answers to them. You might need to do some research too.

- What are the steps you need to take to get there?
- What are the resources you need to get for myself?
- What are the impending obstacles?
- How can you overcome these obstacles?
- Who can help you to achieve your goals? How can you approach them?
- What are the elements that are holding you back?

_____

_____

Once, you have these long-term goals in place, break them into daily, weekly, and monthly goals to keep track of them. Use the following template to help you make notes of your goals and whether you have achieved them.

Daily Goals Worksheet

Before retiring to bed each night, complete this daily goals worksheet:

My goal for tomorrow is:

_____

_____

What steps are needed to ensure these goals are reached?

_____

_____

Weekly Goals Worksheet

Typically, you must complete this either on Sunday night or Monday morning depending on your lifestyle. It would be even better if you could complete it by Saturday night before you set out for your weekend socializing so that you don't forget about it.

My goals for the upcoming week are

_____

_____

What steps are needed to ensure these goals are reached?

_____

_____

Like this, you can make monthly goals and yearly goals as well. Here are some classic examples of goals for men:

- **Health goals:** I want to lose 20 pounds by the end of the half-year. To achieve this, I will exercise every day, keep track of my food intake, and get myself a good health insurance.
- **Creative goals:** I want to pursue my hobby of playing

the guitar. To achieve this, I will join classes from this week, and allocate 30 minutes each day towards my practice.

- **Spiritual goals:** I will meditate 15 minutes every day starting from today. I will volunteer at the orphanage or old age home every second Sunday of the month
- **Financial goals:** I will start saving $500 every month starting from this month. That will ensure I have $6000 of my own money at the end of the year.
-

Chapter Summary

In this chapter, you learned the importance of goal-setting, and how to match your goals to your core values. This chapter also includes worksheet templates you can use for your goal-setting process.

Chapter 6: Tips and Tricks to Build Confidence - Part I

This and the next chapters are dedicated to giving you tips and tricks to build confidence.

Building Confidence through Visualizations

Visualization is nothing but daydreaming with a sense of purpose. Richard Bach, the famous author said, *"To bring anything into your life, imagine that it's already there."* Visualization is a powerful tool to help crystallize dreams.

Arnold Schwarzenegger used visualization techniques to realize his body-building dreams. His role model was Reg Park, the famous English bodybuilder of the 1950s. Arnold said that he kept visualizing himself with his role model's body and was motivated to commit himself wholeheartedly to achieve his dream.

How does visualization help us realize our dreams? Multiple research studies have shown that when we imagine a scene in our heads, the primal parts of our brain behave like the imaginary scene was really happening. Imaginations are known to affect our central nervous system directly.

Therefore, you experience an inexplicable feeling of dread even when you merely imagine yourself facing dangers. Similarly, when you imagine yourself sitting on a beach enjoying the beautiful blue sea, you feel a sense of peace and calmness. Here are some excellent benefits of using visualization techniques to build confidence:

- It activates your subconscious mind to generate excellent ideas to help you achieve your goals
- It programs your brain to quickly and effectively identify and attract resources that can help you achieve your goals.
- The repeated practice of visualization technique helps activate the law of attraction drawing people, resources, and other useful elements into your life.
- It enhances motivation and confidence

Thus, it makes sense to use visualization to increase your confidence levels. Here is an example you can use as a template for visualization exercises in your life:

Visualization Exercise: Suppose you need to ask your boss for a raise. You are feeling nervous and your confidence levels are low, and yet, you know you deserve the raise. Here is what you can do to get rid of nervousness and build your confidence levels before approaching your boss:

First, prepare what you will say to your boss starting from the greeting stage. Make sure you have substantial data about your achievements and solid reasons why you believe you deserve the raise. Practice your speech well.

- Find a quiet place where you will not be disturbed. Sit comfortably.
- Close your eyes and take a deep breath.
- Visualize yourself walking confidently to your boss' cabin and knocking on the door.
- Imagine him giving you permission to enter
- Visualize greeting him confidently and tell him that you have something important to discuss.
- Visualize your boss offering you a seat.
- Imagine giving the prepared speech calmly and confidently. Rehearse the speech in your visualization exercise.
- Visualize your boss giving you a smile and telling you that he agrees with your views.

Keep imagining this happy sequence. Visualizing does not guarantee the exact same outcome in reality. However, repeated visualization helps to eliminate nervousness which, in turn, builds confidence. It is like rehearsing for a play. The more skilled you become, the more confident you get.

Confidence Building through Affirmations

Affirmations are not just mantras to make you feel better. They have the power to make your dreams come true. Affirmations encourage you to lead a more fulfilling and meaningful life than before. Here are some excellent benefits of using affirmations to build confidence:

- Daily affirmations enhance your ability to become acutely aware of your thoughts and emotions thereby preventing negativities from creeping in.
- Your thoughts and actions synchronize with each other, resulting in increased efficiency and productivity.
- Affirmations draw things that you desire into your life, and bring in a lot of divine blessings.
- Affirmations keep you aware of and grateful for the seemingly small elements in your life that bring you a lot of joy and happiness. In the mad rush of the modern world, we tend to forget little things that truly matter in our lives including the joy of loved ones, the comforts of a beautiful home, a healthy body, and more.
- Affirmations help you remain positive which, in turn, builds confidence.

- Affirmations keep your focused and motivated.

Here are some excellent confidence-building affirmations you can try daily. In fact, start your day with an affirmation, and end your day with another.

- I am fearless.
- I am mindful, calm, and confident.
- I am always trying to get better. But, today, I am happy with what I have.
- I am a positive person, and I believe in my capabilities.
- I am compassionate with others and with myself.
- I have the confidence to overcome all obstacles.
- I love to meet new people and have conversations with them.
- I am wise, strong, and powerful.
- I am complete by myself.
- I am my best friend and my best source of motivation.
- Life is beautiful, and I am happy to live it to the fullest.
- Challenges help me grow and learn.
- I am a positive man, and therefore, attract only positive people to myself.
- I am unique, and that's what gives me a strong individuality.
- I make a difference even if I simply turn out each day and

give my best.
- Each day, I am becoming better than yesterday.
- I deserve my desires because I have the capabilities to achieve them, and I work hard for them.
- I am focused on solutions. Obstacles do not deter me.
- I am confident of successfully completing my responsibilities and tasks.
- I love myself, and I look for the best in every situation.
- I am very happy to receive compliments because I know I deserve them.
- I feel grateful for my life and all its offerings.
- Everything is possible provided I am willing to work hard and commit myself.
- I am an open person and I love to look at things in new perspectives.
- I am intelligent and talented.
- I am confident and enthusiastic.
- I am not afraid of making mistakes.

Whenever you feel your confidence ebbing, get away to a quiet and undisturbed place, and repeat your favorite affirmations for a couple of minutes. The problem you had will not go away with affirmations. But your will and resolve to overcome the problem will be multiplied.

Challenge Yourself Continuously

Challenging yourself continuously is the most effective way for self-improvement. If what you are doing does not challenge you and your capabilities, then you are not growing. You are stagnating, which is the first step to downfall. Staying in your comfort zone is the biggest hurdle to building confidence. The longer you remain in your comfort zone, the more complacent you get. The more complacent you get, the more difficult it is to get out of your comfort zone.

The Lotus Eaters in Greek mythology is a classic example of people who were so complacent in their comfort zone that they died even before they started to live. They forgot everything else except to eat the lotus. They stagnated and died on that island. A similar thing can happen to you if you don't get outside of your comfort zone and challenge yourself continually.

Challenging yourself, accomplishing new projects and tasks, doing unfamiliar activities, taking tough decisions, getting physically and mentally uncomfortable, and other such activities are excellent ways of building confidence. Help others as much as you can. However, before helping others, help yourself.

Build your skill sets. Become a master in multiple domains, and you will find yourself becoming increasingly confident with each new skill you acquire. Every time you learn a new skill, you are challenging yourself, and raising the bar for self-improvement. Here are some excellent tips to continuously challenge yourself:

Do something you dislike – If you hate washing dishes, and your wife is constantly nagging you to do it, then give in to her nagging, and wash dishes without complaining for a week. Promise yourself this, and each time you want to complain, remember the promise, and consciously stop yourself from whining. Instead, get off the couch and wash the dishes. It is possible that your wife is going to be super surprised and will want to return the favor in a way you like.

Another example is if you don't like talking to a particular colleague, make an effort for a week to start the conversation with him or her. If you hate to dance, learn dancing. If you don't like to cook, make an effort to help your wife in the kitchen.

What is your biggest fear? Live with it for a week – For example, if you are afraid of change, begin to tackle this fear by making changes in your daily routine. Instead of having breakfast after your bath, have a bath after you eat simply because it is different from your normal routine and will result in making you uncomfortable.

If you are scared to speak in public, use every opportunity you get to speak in front of other people. If you are scared of embarrassment, then try singing loudly or doing something embarrassing in front of people whom you trust. Slowly, the fear will fade. If you are scared of a particular relative, invite him home for a week.

What is your biggest love? Stay away from it for a week – If you love your daily Netflix movie indulgence, then uninstall the app for a week. If you love Facebook or any other social media platform, uninstall the apps for a while.

Do things differently - If you are a left-handed person, then eat with your right hand, and vice versa. If you brush your teeth with your right hand, use your left hand for a week.

Basically, don't allow yourself to feel comfortable. The less comfortable you feel, the more alert you will be. You will be able to garner a lot of skills with this attitude, resulting in improved confidence.

Journals for Confidence Building

Stephen R. Covey, the author of the best-selling book, "The Seven Habits of Highly Effective People," and many others, said, "Keeping a personal journal a daily in-depth analysis and evaluation of your experiences is a high-leverage activity that increases self-awareness and enhances all the endowments and the synergy among them." There are multiple benefits to maintaining a journal. Some of them include:

- Journaling helps you have clarity on your goals and their statuses.
- Journaling helps in daily recovery as you write down and let go of all the emotions of the day.
- Journaling helps you weed out inconsistencies in your life.
- Journaling enhances the power of your learning as you make notes of your daily experiences.
- Journaling helps you keep track of your daily, weekly, and monthly goals. This activity gives you opportunities to tweak and make changes to your goals whenever.
- Journaling improves your sense of gratitude

All these benefits directly impact your confidence levels. In addition to making journal entries of your daily experience, you can make write down positive thoughts to counter confidence-depleting negative thoughts. Here are a few examples for you:

Negative thought: 'I cannot do this.'

- ***Journal prompt #1:*** Make a list of all your achievements right from your school days until last week.

- ***Journal prompt #2:*** Write down an experience which entailed a similar situation. You thought you couldn't do it, but you not only completed it but also did it well.
- ***Journal prompt #3:*** What is the most courageous thing you ever did?

Negative thought: 'I have poor knowledge.'

- ***Journal prompt #1:*** Make a list of subjects where you have excellent knowledge levels. Include the number of hours you have spent learning that topic. What kinds of training you have had? How you have used that knowledge successfully?
- ***Journal prompt #2:*** Make a list of the things you will do to increase your currently poor knowledge levels

Negative thought: 'I think I am very ugly or very fat, and I don't like my looks.'

- ***Journal prompt #1:*** What are you happy about in your body? List at least two things.
- ***Journal prompt #2:*** Make a list of things you are grateful for in your physical body. It can be something as simple as your flexibility, the way your fingers are shaped, your smile, or anything else

- ***Journal prompt #3:*** What are the compliments you have received for your looks?

Negative thought: 'I lack good qualities.'

- ***Journal prompt #1:*** List the things you are grateful in yourself.
- ***Journal prompt #2:*** List the top two compliments you have got from people.
- ***Journal prompt #3:*** What does your best friend think of you?
- ***Journal prompt #4:*** What do you like about yourself?

Negative thought: 'I will definitely fail, therefore I will not try it.'

Journal prompt #1: List the good things that will happen if you DON'T fail.

Journal prompt #2: Make a note of the worst-case scenario. Now, find ways to means manage the situation even if this was to happen.

Chapter Summary

In this chapter, you learned three different ways to build confidence including using visualization techniques, affirmations, challenging yourself, and journaling.

Chapter 7: Tips and Tricks to Build Confidence - Part II

Avoid Perfectionism

Perfection is only an excuse for self-criticism. Even gold in its perfect form can never be made into beautiful jewelry. It needs a bit of imperfection in the form of copper to create stunning artwork. You are motivated by striving for excellence whereas you feel demoralized if you strive for perfection. Leo Tolstoy said, *"If you look for perfection, you will never find contentment and happiness."*

Trying your best to do a job well is a healthy attitude to have. Being obsessed with perfectionism is a dangerously unhealthy trait to have. Perfectionism is one of the primary obstacles of confidence building. An obsessive perfectionist is plagued by these negative and debilitating thoughts and emotions:

- I don't like the way I am at present.
- I never seem to be satisfied with anything.
- I see the entire world and all it's happening in black and white. I cannot forgive myself or anybody else for being grey which is the color of the realistic world.
- I think if I achieve perfection I will be at peace.

- I have to constantly overachieve to feel even a small amount of satisfaction.
- If I don't get exactly what I set my mind to, I complain and whine.
- Efforts and intentions are never enough. I should see tangible and flawless results.

What happens if you try to be a perfectionist? Here are some challenges that will negatively impact your daily life, making it miserable and unlivable:

You are always anxious and tired – In your efforts to overachieve and better yourself each time, you will be in a constant state of high-alert, leading to excessive stress, fatigue, and anxiety. Also, the incremental energy needed to take a job well done to a 'perfect' level is significantly larger than what you used to reach the level of excellence. The incremental benefit is not worthy of this effort. Thus, perfection uses up excessive energy needlessly.

Unhappy relationships - Driven by the stress of your unreasonable expectations, people who are in a relationship with you will always feel anxious and worried. This kind of worry can easily ruin a relationship sooner rather than later. You are constantly finding fault with your wife or partner which can drive her crazy, and she is bound to walk out.

Similarly, your unreasonable expectations from your children can make them either fear you or hate you as a father. Relationships from all sides are bound to suffer if you are obsessed with perfection.

You will always feel guilty or ashamed of yourself – Perfectionists look at the outside world as a reflection of their inner self. So, if you are a perfectionist and you see a mess, clutter, or disorganization around you, you transfer that mess and clutter into yourself. This outlook fills them with shame and guilt for not doing your job well which is not the true picture. Therefore, you are always plagued by a sense of guilt and shame. Instead of trying to be Mr. Perfect, make sure you have given your best at everything, and leave it at that. Here are some tips to help you overcome the obsession over perfection:

Know that perfectionism is a myth – Perfectionism, like all things in this world, is relative. What is perfect for you could be just be good enough for someone else, and vice versa. Also, in your own life, the concept of perfectionism is different for different aspects. For example, at your work, you could expect perfection from your subordinates whereas at home you could choose to be slack with your kids. Therefore, accept that perfectionism is only in your head, and is not possible in real life.

Learn to accept being good enough – Accepting good enough is not slacking off from doing your best. It only means to give up obsessing over perfection. We can find a good-enough level for all the work we do. Don't waste precious time and energy resources to following up with perfectionism.

For example, if your office presentation for monthly sales has come out accurately and up to expectations, then don't feel the unnecessary pressure of being the expert mathematician and try to get the numbers perfectly right up to the 6th decimal place! Let it be and go with the accurate figures.

Accept that human beings are imperfect and will make mistakes – Human beings are imperfect, and our world is full of flaws. Things are bound to go wrong sometimes. Accept mistakes as learning opportunities and move on.

And finally, the people who matter in your life will never reject you for human imperfections. In fact, your loved ones will love you more for your mistakes because it makes you more human and endearing. Of course, these tips to avoid perfectionism does not mean you don't try to do your best. It is only to help you overcome your obsession with perfectionism.

Love Yourself

The relationship you share with yourself sets the tone for every other relationship you have or will have with others. Oscar Wilde said, *'To love oneself is the beginning of a lifelong, never-ending romance.'*

Loving yourself does not mean being narcissistic or self-centered. It only means you identify, respect, and accept yourself the way you are and for what you are. Self-love is a quality that gives us control over our own lives while teaching us to be compassionate towards everyone starting from ourselves.

Here are some great benefits of loving ourselves:
- We are free from greed, anger, and resentment because we wholeheartedly accept ourselves the way we are, and therefore, we don't find ourselves wanting anything.
- We are free from the worry about how others perceive us because it doesn't matter to us anymore.
- We are free from having to maintain a façade for the sake of the outside world. Our behavior becomes authentic.
- We love our own company and don't feel lonely when we are alone.
- We are free from fear because we know we are always there for ourselves.

- We take control of our lives as we realize that only we are responsible for bringing joy and happiness for ourselves.

How can we love ourselves? Here are some tips for you:

List all the good things in your life – The list of good things in your life helps you perceive your life positively. You focus on the elements that make you happy. This attitude makes you realize the abundance of joy in your life. When you realize this abundance, you learn yourself and your life more.

Surround yourself with people who love you – While self-love is very important, sometimes we need people to reiterate their love for us to feel good and happy. Create a loving social circle around yourself filled with people who care for and like you and will not hesitate to say so when you are down and depressed.

Maintain a clean and hygienic lifestyle – Remove physical, mental, and emotional clutter from your life. Maintain a clean, negativity-free, and clutter-free lifestyle. This attitude will give you a sense of freedom, happiness, and lightness that is in stark contrast to the feeling of heaviness that comes with a cluttered, negativity-filled, and disorganized lifestyle.

Use these self-love practices daily:
- Start your day with a self-love affirmation.

- Respect and love your body.
- Don't take your thoughts seriously. Many of them, especially the negative ones, come only to scare and confuse you.
- You are unique. Therefore, don't ever compare yourself with anyone else.
- Be proud of your achievements.
- Keep away from all kinds of toxicity from your life. Avoid people who demoralize you, think you are useless, mistreat you, etc.

Have a Positive Attitude

Confucius said, 'To put the world right in order, we must first put the nation in order; to put the nation in order, we must first put the family in order; to put the family in order, we must first cultivate our personal life; we must first set our hearts right.'

Keep a positive attitude if you want to build confidence. The more positive you are, the more positive elements come into your life. Here are some great benefits to having a positive attitude:

Challenges become opportunities – When you see everything in a positive light, then challenges become opportunities for your development, and not obstacles to stifle your growth. When you see opportunities instead of challenges, you will find creative solutions that bring you success. Increased success translates to increased confidence.

Increased motivation – With a positive attitude, you feel motivated to give your best resulting in increased chances of success which, in turn, enhance confidence and self-esteem.

Reduction in stress levels – Negative thoughts and attitudes fill your mind with stress and anxiety. A positive outlook reduces the level of stress because you choose to focus on the good things. Therefore, you can use your energy to do productive work instead of using it to manage undue stress and anxiety.

Here are some tips to build a positive attitude:

Live in the moment – Worrying about the past and future leads to unnecessary negativity. You are wasting your time and energy regretting the past and thinking about an uncertain future. Living in the moment empowers you to experience life fully and fills you with a positive feeling.

Use positive words to describe yourself and your life – Our choice of words have a powerful impact on our lives. If we use negative words to describe our life, then that is how you perceive it. For example, if you say, 'My job is boring, mundane, and busy,' then that is how your job is. However, if you say, 'My job is exciting, unique, and different,' then your job becomes that. The situation does not impact your life as much as your response to it. Therefore, always use positive words to bring positivity into your life.

Replace 'have' with 'get' – Here are some examples:
- 'I have to pay rent' must become 'I get to pay rent.'
- 'I have to go to work' must become 'I get to go to work.'

The sentence with the 'have' sounds obligatory whereas the sentence with 'get' sounds like an opportunity. One simple change of word results in perceiving things positively.

Surround yourself with positive people always, and be conscious of your every action, thought, and response so that you can choose to be positive rather than negative. Surround yourself with confident people. Don't be jealous of their confidence. Simply learn from them and imbibe their qualities into your life.

Chapter Summary

In this chapter, you learned how to build confidence by avoid perfectionism, loving and respecting yourself, and having a positive attitude.

Chapter 8: Conclusion

The main takeaways from this book include:

- Building confidence begins with your simple decision to wake up each morning and promise yourself that you will be confident today.
- Understand your current level of confidence so that you know what you need to do next to get better at it.
- Create a growth mindset and learn to master skills you are not good at.
- Create your core values based on your life experiences. Understanding your core values helps you relate openly and honestly with your strengths and weaknesses.
- Use your core values and create goals for your life. The absence of clear goals and a life purpose will constantly throw you into a confused state of mind. With clearly established goals and life purposes, you are absolutely certain of the life path you need to take to achieve your goals. This sense of certainty boosts your confidence level significantly.
- Knowing and identifying your goals empowers you to live your life on your terms and not be worried about what others think.
- Tips and tricks on how to build confidence in your life.

So, go ahead, and start your confidence building journey today! Confidence is closely related to assertiveness and self-esteem.

When the value of one increases, the value of the other two also goes up in your life.

There are two other books by the same author titled 'Self-Esteem for Men' and 'Assertiveness for Men.' that deal with assertiveness and self-esteem in the same way this book deals with confidence.

The complete titles from John Adams:
Self Esteem for Men: 5 Simple but Overlooked Methods to Start Your Inner Journey and Which Will Stop You from Being a Doormat
Confidence for Men: 3 Secret Hacks to Live Life on Your Terms
Read them to get a complete overhaul of your life.

www.ingramcontent.com/pod-product-compliance
Lightning Source LLC
Chambersburg PA
CBHW052120110526
44592CB00013B/1693